MILLENNIAL VS. MACHINE

HOW I GOT SOMEONE ELSE TO PAY OFF MY STUDENT LOAN DEBT AND HOW YOU CAN DO THE SAME!

COURTNEY M. KING

COURTNEY M. KING

DEDICATION

As I sit here writing this dedication, I can't help but think of the scripture, "Honor your father and mother" (which is the first commandment with a promise), that it may go well with you and that you may have a long life on the earth." Ephesians 6:2-3 NIV

This book is dedicated to my parents David and Stacie.

Dad, thank you for always pushing me to pursue the Kingdom of God, and thank you for the opportunity to work alongside you in real estate and in life!

Mom, thank you for reminding me at every waking hour that I needed to go to college lol. And thank you for always stressing the importance of fiscal responsibility and a positive credit score.

CONTENTS

ACKNOWLEDGEMENT

Matthew 6:33 says "But seek first the kingdom of God and His righteousness, and all these things shall be added to you." ESV

I write this to acknowledge God's Kingdom and His righteousness FIRST before we dive into this book. He is my author and finisher and I'm so thankful that He gave me the words and instructions to write this book! May His kingdom come and His will be done on earth as it is in heaven. Amen.

INTRODUCTION

Student loan debt has my fellow millennials underwater! THIS BOOK IS FOR YOU!!! They (the world, our parents, our society) say, "go to college, get a job and build a career!" While that was sound advice rooted in love and the desire for us to go even further than our parents, it still doesn't solve the problem of the massive amount of student loan debt that many college grads, including myself, have when completing their undergraduate studies. This book shares my experience of how one can get someone else to pay off their student loan debt when the income of a 9 to 5 just doesn't cut it. Keep in mind that this book doesn't constitute any legal or financial advice.

Additionally, while I am a Texas real estate Broker, this book does not establish any sort of broker/agent representation. This is, in fact just my story and the advice that my dad passed to me! I hope this story will help you to overcome the machine of student loans and live in financial freedom.

1

MILLENNIAL VS. MACHINE

Let me start, with thank you for picking up this book! If you are like me, you are actively pursuing financial freedom; in particular, freedom from Sallie Mae and all student loan debt!

I am a millennial and first-generation college graduate! I'm my parent's oldest child, and from a young age (and daily), my mom would remind me "You're going to college!" My mom was a cake decorator, and my dad, having dropped out of high school, was a general contractor and serial entrepreneur. With that being said, while I knew I was going to college, I had NO idea how or how I (keyword I) was going to pay for it since my family wasn't in any financial situation to pay for it.

In April of 2007, I graduated with bachelor's degrees in political science and Spanish. "How did you do it?" you ask! Well, on the one hand I received various scholarships, but on the other hand, I had to take out some student loans. After all, the grants and scholarships only went so far, with $40,000 per year tuition. While I planned to become a high-powered attorney and get a job fast so that I could begin paying off my student loans by the time that the 6-month forbearance period was up, God had other plans. As I write this Proverbs 19: 21 comes to mind: "Many are the plans in a person's heart, but it is the LORD's purpose that prevails." (NIV)

At this point, I was a college grad with approximately $25,000 in student loan debt, no job in sight, and living on a friend's couch! After bombing on the LSATs TWICE and not feeling sure about the law school route, I worked as a project assistant at a commercial real estate law firm and then as a paralegal at an immigration law firm; still holding on to this "dream" of being an attorney and helping people! When the 2008 crash hit, I quickly realized 1) I wanted some stability, and 2) I didn't want to go to law school and rack up even more debt that I had. So, what did I do, you ask. With the advice of my dad, I became a bilingual elementary school teacher. Of course, that was the next logical thing, right? My 3-year journey as a teacher barely making ends meet can be the topic for another book, but during my teaching days I would spend time with my dad who later became a real estate broker and who had successfully built and operated a property management company where I worked at during my holiday and summer breaks during college. The more time I spent with him, the more I saw the freedom he had as well as the money that he was making. In my second year as a teacher, I decided to get my real estate license. After all, a teacher's day ended around 3PM PLUS we had quite a few holidays and the weekends off, and this was when most people were looking for homes.

Hindsight is always 20/20. In my quest to do my "own" thing, I had never considered following in my dad's footsteps and joining the family business, but after thinking about it, I finished my real estate courses during a week spring break in 2010, took my exam and got my real estate license. From there, the rest is HISTORY! While teaching, I took the time to market myself and build a pipeline so that I could successfully transition from my 9 to 5 to full-time real estate in the summer of 2012.

As of this writing, I am a licensed real estate broker in Texas and own and operate King Realty & Management Inc. While it took me a while to figure out "my lane," I'm here, and I love it! I am so happy and motivated to help others achieve their real estate goals and financial freedom through real estate.

In pursuit of freedom from student loans

I'm writing this book because I see a HUGE need for millennials to learn a time-proven approach on how they can leverage what they do have, to alleviate the stress of student loans. And better yet, if you don't have any student loans, you can also use my story to help you tackle other debts and even help you save money too!

As of this writing, the elections of 2020 are in the distant future, and millennials have a significant stake in what takes place. As I see all of the candidates (both democrat and republican) "tackle" this issue, student loan debt seems to be something everyone is talking about, BUT I don't see any real action. Additionally, the machine, which is student loan lending, is SO large. I honestly don't think that the issues can be solved by politicians! Hosea 4:6 says, "My people are destroyed for lack of knowledge." I firmly believe KNOWLEDGE is the key to overcoming the machine! I hope that by sharing the gems that my father passed to me, you can do the same and experience freedom.

How to use this book

Take a ride with me in my journey of getting someone else to pay off my student loan debt. I hope that after reading this, you will be inspired to learn more about how to do it in your local real estate market and teach your children the same thing so that they are not bound by student loan debt in the future.

If you don't have any student loan debt, but other liabilities like credit card debt, private loans, or lines of credit, these same strategies that I discuss here can be used to tackle those and more!

As I reflect on where my parents started (from an educational and financial standpoint), to where I am now, I see a TON of growth! I'm so thankful for my dad's guidance as a young adult to now, and I hope that by sharing my experience, I can help others my age, my younger siblings, and my future kids live in financial freedom. I pray the same for you too! Let's jump right into the journey.

2

STUDENT LOAN DEBT IN THE UNITED STATES

One of the most commonly held perspectives in the United States culture, (especially among my generation), is that after high school, you go to college, and after college you get a good job. Even as I was growing up, I would see people look down on those that didn't go to college.

While that was what I heard in my household and in middle and high schools, the one thing nobody ever talked about what how to pay for college; no talk about preparing for that expense or even what to do. I mean, after all, you would have a good job after college, so maybe that explains why there was never a discussion?

In my experience, there was an unwritten/unspoken agreement that my parents, while there to help in the ways they could, weren't able to finance my education. As a result, my last year and a half of high school were ALL about scholarships. But again, there was no guarantee that that would cover everything or that I would even receive the scholarships that I applied for.

Being a first-generation soon-to-be college student, I didn't even consider the possibility of not using the degrees I received after the four-year journey! So much for the philosophy "Go to college get a degree and make a lot of money."

Student loans in the United States

According to an NBC news article from April 2019, one in five adult Americans (approximately 44.7 million people) carries student loan debt.[1] According to the Federal Reserve Bank of New York, at the end of 2018 the total amount of student loan debt was $1.47 trillion, which is more than credit cards or auto loans.[2]

The figure[3] below shows the average debt that most borrowers carry. Most borrowers have between $10,000-$25,000 in student loan debt, which is where I fell after I graduated.

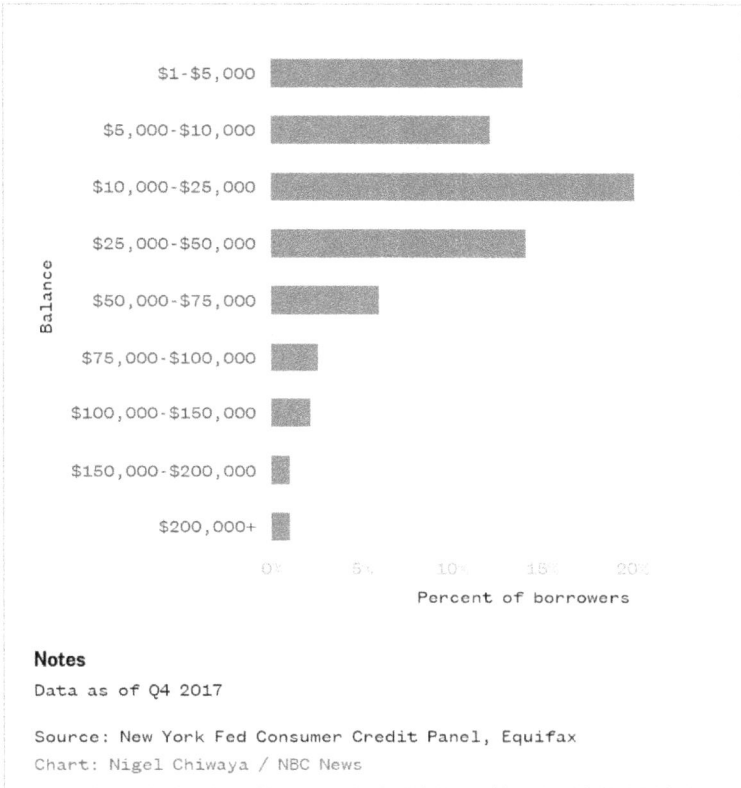

Notes

Data as of Q4 2017

Source: New York Fed Consumer Credit Panel, Equifax

Chart: Nigel Chiwaya / NBC News

Without getting TOO political, the government borrows this money at a meager interest rate and then lends it to students a higher interest rate, and that's how they make money on student loans. In a May 2014 report by the Congressional Budget Office, they projected "earnings" (or rather budget savings depending on how you look at it) of $135 billion over the next decade by way of the student loan programs[4]. It's a giant machine that is enveloping everyone in its path, and there are no apparent signs of an end.

What does it mean for the average Joe or Jane like us?

It's pretty clear from the data you just read and even from simple conversations with your friends and family, that student loan debt is a problem. To start, the excitement of college graduation quickly fades at the thought of the repayment period beginning within six months. When I graduated, I was so pressed to get a job (any job at that) because I knew I would have to start paying them back very soon. This stress seemed to discount all that I worked for in my undergraduate career and thus make the focus money instead of purpose. On top of that, at the time that I graduated, I was living in Los Angeles, California which is one of the most expensive places to live in the United States. While I did end up getting a "good" job as a project assistant at a local law firm, with rent and expenses I was living paycheck to paycheck! I had a dream to drive a nice car and own a home, and I quickly knew that in Los Angeles that wouldn't be a possibility unless I married someone rich (and that didn't seem imminent either). I was beginning to lose hope and become miserable, to say the least. Without a clear idea of next steps, I talked to my dad who was investing in Real Estate in my hometown of Portland, Oregon and in the Dallas-Fort Worth, Texas area. After a quick visit to Dallas and a talk with my dad I knew I had to leave L.A., so I moved to Dallas about 1-year after graduation (Spring of 2008).

3

MY "FIGHT" AGAINST THE MACHINE OF STUDENT LOANS

In Spring 2007, I found myself jobless, living in an expensive city and the looming student loan repayment off in the near future (six months to be exact!). At the end of my undergraduate career, I had approximately $25,000 in federal and private loans in my name. Talk about stressed! Not to mention, I still didn't have a clear vision for my life or genuinely understand my purpose.

As I had mentioned, I left Los Angeles and moved to Dallas in early 2008, where I would continue my journey as a paralegal at an immigration law firm. The economy of the United States TANKED during the mortgage crisis and recession of 2008. What did this mean for me? The law firm I was at was experiencing financial difficulty, and I had a decision to make. Do I stay on board, or do I take some preventative steps to ensure that I didn't end where I left off after college, jobless? After more talks with my dad (did I mention Dads are the best!), he asked if I had considered teaching. After all, I was fluent in Spanish, and there was a significant need for bilingual teachers. Of course, my first thought was "NO, I hadn't considered it" and my second thought was "YES!!! Let's do it.... good, stable, government job." While there was still a small desire to be an attorney, at that point in the economy many people my age and older were going back to school (graduate school...law school included) because that's all they could do with the active recession. At the end of the day, all I could see was the possibility of additional student loan debt and an oversaturation of the already saturated market of practicing attorneys. Needless to say, I quickly entered into an alternative teaching certification program and became a bilingual elementary school teacher. After my first year of teaching I felt confident and comfortable. I was a w2 employee with stable income and a pretty cushy work schedule. Because of the flexibility in my work schedule and as a result of seeing how successful my dad was as a real estate agent and then broker, in 2010 (while still a teacher), I got my real estate license. To learn more about my story as a real estate agent and how you can also become a thriving real estate agent please visit www.CourtneyMKing.com.

One weekend I was spending time with my dad, and we went to show a house to a buyer (client) that he was working with. As we walked through the property, the buyer picked apart every last detail of the home. She saw a dump! My dad, on the other hand, saw an AMAZING opportunity. My dad would later help her find another home, but after that showing we hopped in the car, and a lightbulb began to go off.

My dad asked, "Courtney, do you want to buy this home? It would be a perfect rental property!" Utterly terrified, I began to blurt out a ton of questions. "How much would it cost to fix up? How much would my mortgage be? How much..." At that season in my life, I was all about the numbers and spreadsheets, calculating EVERY, and I mean EVERY move! I couldn't see the opportunity. All I saw was fear. My dad took notice. He concluded the conversation with, "Well if you don't want to buy it, I will!" That's ALL he had to say. You see, my dad has been such a large part of my life and had always guided me into good things and sound decisions. When he said that, with fear and all, I committed to buying the home. I understood that his advice was always sound and that while I couldn't see the full vision of what it could be, my dad could, and that's all I needed.

The opportunity

When I got the opportunity to purchase this home on Michael Drive, I had the credit score to qualify for financing, and I learned that as a w2 employee, it was SUPER easy to get financed. In chapter 4, we will discuss the overall financial position that would be conducive for you to capitalize on an opportunity like this one.

I closed on the purchase in May 2011. Michael Drive was 4 bedrooms, 2 baths, built-in 1977, and 1,929 square feet. I purchased the property for $68,000 (yes, you read that correctly). My mortgage on this property was approximately $630 per month which included taxes and insurance. There are different loan products, and of course, interest rates fluctuate so we won't get into the specifics of the loan, but feel free to visit www.CourtneyMKing.com/start for more details on this.

Because the property was in an area that had consistently high demand and somewhat desirable schools (we'll talk later about how to identify these things), I was able to get it rented quickly for $1295 per month. What did this mean? I cash flowed $665 per month. In layman's terms, what the tenant paid in monthly rent covered the mortgage AND allowed me to put $665 per month in my pocket. Over one year, that ended up producing a gross income of $7,980. Since I had a job that allowed me to cover all of my living expenses,

I would let the monthly cash-flow stack up in a separate account. HOWEVER, for you, this may be an opportunity to have the asset (the house and the monthly cash flow produced) to cover your liability (monthly student loan payment). If you don't have student loan debt, but you have credit card debt, you could use this cash flow to pay down or pay off any other debt.

I have just highlighted the cashflow benefits of this rental property; however, I can't neglect the tax benefits. Keep in mind I am not a CPA or offering any tax advice, but from experience, I have learned that while this home was producing additional income for me, it was also producing tax deductions. One of the biggest deductions was the depreciation deduction (structure value only/27.5 years = total annual depreciation). PLUS I was also able to deduct my rental expenses like repairs, make-readies, property management fees, and commissions related to leasing the property. This offset my overall taxable income. If you are considering the strategies I've highlighted in this book, be sure to do your own due diligence and talk with your CPA or tax advisor before moving forward.

How someone else paid off my student loans

This book is all about how someone else paid off my student loans. "Who is that someone else?" you ask. That someone else was my tenant and later the client that bought the property from me. I leveraged my good credit and my job to help me finance the purchase of the property. Then I used the monthly cash flow to pay my monthly student loan debt. It gets even better!

By early summer 2012, I had an opportunity to leave my career as an elementary school teacher and join my family's real estate brokerage full-time as a licensed real estate agent.

Despite the fear of leaving a stable teaching job, I dove right in!

One year later, a long-term client of my dad was looking for a rental property to purchase. Did I mention dads are the best? He talked with me and asked if I wanted to consider selling Michael Drive and thus pay off the rest of my student loans with the proceeds and put some money in my pocket. I was 100% on board! In early 2013 I sold the property for a net profit of over $20,000 (in less than two years since I originally purchased it.

In the next chapters, I will walk you step-by-step on how you can leverage yourself to purchase an asset (a rental property) and allow someone else (your tenant) to pay off your liability (student loans or other debt). Are you ready to start the journey?

4
_____

EXAMINING YOUR SITUATION AND SETTING GOALS

The first step in the process of getting someone else to pay off your student loans through leverage/real estate is to look at your current financial situation. From a young age, my parents stressed how important good credit is and how to be a good steward of the money I earned. To continue the conversation about money management and being a good steward of your finances, be sure to visit www. CourtneyMKing.com/money. One of the best pieces of advice that I got from my dad while in my 2nd semester of college was to get a credit card and to use it for my gas and groceries only and to pay it off in full each month. If you're a parent reading this book, make sure you really talk to your child about the why and the how. A conversation about discipline and fiscal responsibility is critical and shouldn't be overlooked. This advice from my dad enabled me to graduate college with a 700+ credit score, which would later help me buy the Michael Drive home.

If you have significant debt and/or a low credit score, it would be a good idea to reach out to a personal finance professional to examine your current status, collaborate on a savings plan and implement practical steps to help you increase your credit score.

Aside from credit, your income and employment is the next key to being able to finance the purchase of this investment property. Believe it or not, w2 employees have the easiest time to get financed. As a teacher, when I purchased the home on Michael Drive, I was surprised at how easy it was to get approved for the mortgage with little money down. Of course, lending requirements and loan products vary based on the economy. As you read this book, if you have any questions about financing be sure to visit www. CourtneyMKing.com/start, and I am happy to refer you to qualified lending professionals that can further guide you.

I understand that the financing piece of this process is likely the scariest. Will I be approved? Do you have a high enough credit score? Will they even lend to me? Are all questions that ran through my head and may run through yours. The fact of the matter is that you won't know until you try and you won't get any answers until you ask. Lenders are not there to judge; after all, they are looking to close the deal. Many lenders that I have dealt with will not only look at your current financial situation but also offer lots of valuable advice. If you're where you need to be and can get financed for the purchase of this investment, great! If not, there's room for growth and to work your way to getting in the right position to obtain financing.

Goal setting

Before I jump right into goal setting, let's talk about discipline. We can set all kinds of goals, but without discipline, you won't see any progress. One thing that may promote our discipline is breaking our broad goals down into smaller, more manageable goals. Knowing yourself, along with your money habits, may help you understand how that will help you stick to your goals. Also, there are a TON of free online resources and mobile apps that will help you with this. If you want accountability partners or to work with like-minded individuals looking to CRUSH their student loan debt, be sure to join our private community at www. CourtneyMKing.com/join.

In terms of my goals, I like to break them down into long-term and short-term goals. One of my goals with the purchase of Michael Drive was to use the cash flow to pay my monthly student loan payment (short-term). Another goal was to pay my student loans off in full with the proceeds from future sale of the property (long-term). Your goals may be the same or similar. Of course, I created these goals to be SMART (specific, measurable, achievable, relevant, timebound). As you draft your goals, be sure to look at the overall student loan debt (or other liabilities if you want to use this to tackle other debt) you carry. Next, look at your current financial situation. If your credit is good, but you don't have enough money to put down, then maybe you start with savings goals, taking into account your monthly income and how much you can realistically save per month OR what expense you can cut to achieve your savings goals. If you have enough in savings for your down payment but don't have the credit needed to get financed be sure to include that as one of your short-term goals.

When it comes to long term goals, investing in real estate is a LONG game! It is not a get rich quick thing. With my Michael Drive property, I begin to cashflow immediately because I was able to lease the property very quickly. However, it was one year, eight months, and twenty-nine days until I sold the property and finished paying off my student loan debt. This was about five years from the date that I grad-uated from college. If I had been more aggressive with the payment using the cash flow from the rent, then I could have paid it off sooner. If you're a parent preparing for paying for your kids' college education through investment property, you are ahead of the game!

Market research – Where to invest!

Now that you have an idea of what you are looking to achieve (your SMART goals), let's talk about WHERE to invest. For all of the readers that are on the west coast, I feel your pain! For me, buying an investment property in my hometown of Portland, Oregon or in Los Angeles, California, where I attended undergrad, was IMPOSSIBLE! Luckily my father was already investing in Dallas-Fort Worth, Texas so I knew that was the best route for me. And I continue to invest in both Dallas-Fort Worth and Houston Texas markets. Here's a practical guide to decide where you should invest.

To start, I recommend that you look at the market where you currently live. It's important to acknowledge that the real estate market runs as a cycle. As you consider where to buy, it's a good idea to talk with a local real estate professional. They are going to be able to show you where the market is in the cycle and talk about the best time and location to invest. When I purchased Michael Drive, it was shortly after the crash of 2008. It was a downtime where prices were super low, and so were interest rates. Make sure you do your due diligence and talk to other seasoned investors and real estate professionals to better understand the market where you live.

If you are considering investing in the Texas real estate market, I am happy to be a resource to you. As of the writing of this book, the economy in Texas is booming, which is creating a significant demand for rental properties. Additionally, it is still possible to find affordable homes that can be rented out. Be sure to visit www.KingRealtyTx.com/start for more information on how we can help you understand and invest in Texas. If you are considering investing outside of the State of Texas, I am happy to refer you to qualified real estate professionals that can guide you in the process. In the following chapters, I will show you the step-by-step process of how to do what I did with Michael Drive and have someone else pay off my student loan debt.

STEP ONE

FINDING A TEAM

One thing that I have come to learn in my 33 years on this earth is that I NEED HELP! In a culture that is all about DIY, it's essential to know that it is okay to need help, and in fact, you can minimize any troubles ahead of time if you ask for help. Some of you reading this may be entirely new to the idea of investing in real estate, and as a result, your team is vital. Here's a list of your key players!

Real Estate Agent or Broker

As a real estate broker and daughter of a broker/investor, I understand that you have MANY options on who you can select as your agent. It is IMPERATIVE to work with someone that has experience in <u>investing</u>, someone who currently owns or has owned rental property. This is a key because they have the personal experience of what you're trying to achieve with the investment property. They will have the expertise needed as well as an understanding of how an investor thinks and operates.

Mortgage Lender (aka Mortgage Broker)

This is another field that is saturated, which means many lenders are vying for your business. I put the lender as the second on this list because your "investor-friendly" agent or broker is likely going to have great referrals with whom they have done a lot of business.

When it comes to shopping around, you'll want to compare interest rates, loan products, and fees. Aside from the practical, I've found that selecting a mortgage lender that is responsive and replies promptly to your requests or emails is key to having a favorable financing experience. Also, if you're not able to qualify now, a suitable lender will give you tips on what you can do to improve your situation.

Property Manager

In some states, a real estate agent has to have an actual (separate) property management license. If your agent/broker is not an experienced property manager, it is important to look for one. A property manager will assist you in leasing and marketing the property as well as drafting all of the lease documents, ensuring that the property is in compliance, and managing the day-to-day rent collection and maintenance. My brokerage King Realty & Management Inc., assists in acquisition and property management in the Dallas-Fort Worth and Houston Texas markets. When interviewing property managers be sure to ask about their personal experience investing in residential real estate as well as the contact information for a few of their current clients. You can also visit www.KingRealtyTX.com/FAQ for questions that you can use as you interview property managers. Property management can make or break your investment, so it's imperative to carefully weigh their reviews, references and overall system before you decide.

Making contact and getting started

Locating your team may be somewhat time-consuming on the front end; however, it will spare you headaches on the back end. As you reach out to various possible team members, be sure to make your goals clear. If there are ever any questions, be sure to speak up. I remember how daunting the process is in getting started, and I help clients through that every day now as a real estate broker.

Once you select your team, be sure to ask them to send you investment opportunities that fit your goals. In the next chapter, we will talk about how to locate the right opportunity. Just remember, be patient!

One thing that I have left out is how you will purchase the property; meaning will it be in your name or an LLC? Often it is easier to purchase a property under your personal name. It is important to consider asset protection and minimizing liability, but that is beyond the scope of this book. I would recommend that you consult with an attorney as there are so many strategies for asset protection.

STEP TWO

LOCATING THE RIGHT OPPORTUNITY (AND WORKING WITH YOUR TEAM)

Now that you know your goals and you've got your team, the next step is to find the right opportunity. For me, Michael Drive was the perfect opportunity because the price compared to what it would rent for was excellent. Most investors use the 1% rule as a general rule of thumb to decide if an opportunity is worth looking in to. That is, the rental rate must be at least one percent of the total sale price. This "rule" is just a start, a way to quickly weed out opportunities, but it still requires more due diligence.

Most of your opportunities will come from your real estate agent or broker. These are properties listed in the Multiple Listing Service. I think this is a great place to start, especially for someone that does not have any investment experience. Additionally, your agent or broker will likely have other opportunities that may not hit the Multiple Listing Service (MLS) by virtue of networking or their other clients looking to sell. These "off-market" opportunities should also be strongly be considered.

Other avenues where you can locate opportunities would be the Facebook marketplace, which as of the writing of this book, has many options. There are also real estate investor groups on Facebook and a site called Bigger Pockets, where investors promote different opportunities. If you use a source outside of the MLS, be sure to send your agent the specifics of the property. They will still be able to represent you in the purchase (even if it's not on the MLS) and pull reports that will help you determine the overall value and how much you can rent the property for. I will stress this again; you mustn't go at this alone, especially if you don't have any investment experience.

Analyzing the opportunity

I already highlighted the 1% rule, which you can use to quickly identify if a property is worth considering, but it's essential to dive deeper. Because time is precious, I recommend that you look at the property on paper before scheduling a showing. Your agent/broker should pull a sales and leasing report, which shows what similar properties have sold and leased for in the area where the property is located. In Texas, this is called CMA or Comparable Market Analysis. The "comparables" are similar properties in the area that you can use as a guide to determine what properties are renting and selling for. This is important to understand what your offer should be and what your potential cash flow is.

Below is a quick analysis of a potential opportunity. To access your free worksheet, please visit www.CourtneyMK-ing.com/analyze. Keep reading as after you have viewed the property, you will need to factor in make-ready costs as well as closing costs.

EXAMPLE OPPORTUNITY A

Purchase		Rental	
Purchase Price:	$ 100,000	Monthly Rental Rate:	$1,200
Down Payment:	$ 20,000	Monthly Management Fee:	$96.00
Estimated Annual Taxes:	$ 2,600	5% Maintenance:	$60.00
Estimated Annual Insurance:	$ 1,200	5% Vacancy:	$60.00
Estimated Monthly Payment (PITI):	$ 750	Monthly Mortgage Payment (PITI):	$750
		Monthly HOA dues:	0
Doesn't factor in closing costs. Be sure to discuss these cost with your agent as they vary and you may be able to get a seller to pay those.		Estimated Net Monthly Income:	$234.00
		Estimated Net Annual Income:	$2,808.00
		Estimated Annual ROI:	14%

When analyzing an opportunity, it's a good idea to factor in maintenance and vacancy expenses. I usually factor in 5% for each, but with your first investment, you may want to factor in 10% for each. This also varies based on the market. It's wise to factor these in your calculations as the money you set aside for each will help you get through any periods of vacancy or if any maintenance expenses arise.

After you have determined that on paper, the property works, be sure to schedule a showing with your agent. I should not have to say this, but just in case I am going to anyway. DO NOT BUY A PROPERTY SIGHT UNSEEN! Sometimes seasoned investors will do this, and that's okay, but if you are just getting started, be sure to view the property AND have a formal, professional inspection as well.

After you've seen the property, your agent/broker should be able to give you a good idea of the total costs of repairs. If they are not comfortable with giving you a rough estimate on price, be sure to connect with a qualified contractor that can provide you a bid for these items. In Texas, there is option period that allows buyers to complete a professional inspection. You can also get a formal bid during the option period and/or after you've had a professional inspection.

Once you have an idea of the basic "make-ready" needed (e.g., basic repairs so that the property is habitable and in compliance with landlord-tenant laws), you'll need to factor this in your purchase expenses. See the updated analysis worksheet.

EXAMPLE OPPORTUNITY A

Purchase			Rental	
Purchase Price:	$	100,000	Monthly Rental Rate:	$1,200
Down Payment:	$	20,000	Monthly Management Fee:	$96.00
Estimated Annual Taxes:	$	2,600	5% Maintenance:	$60.00
Estimated Annual Insurance:	$	1,200	5% Vacancy:	$60.00
Estimated Monthly Payment (PITI):	$	750	Monthly Mortgage Payment (PITI):	$750
Estimated Make Ready Expenses:	$	1,500	Monthly HOA dues:	0
Estimated Closing costs:	$	2,400.00	**Estimated Net Monthly Income:**	**$234.00**
Total Initial Investment:	$	23,900	**Estimated Net Annual Income:**	**$2,808.00**
			ADJUSTED Estimated Annual ROI:	12%

Now that you've determined which opportunity you want to pursue, it's time to work hand-in-hand with your agent on making an offer. Here are a few tips!

1. Stick to your goals and figures. Even though I have purchased many investment properties since Michael Drive, I still feel pressure to "settle" or go against the numbers that I have analyzed. Especially in a hot market where there is competition with other investors, sometimes you

may face having to increase your offer amount just to get your offer accepted. It's a good idea to remain conservative and stick to the figures that you and your agent or broker have discussed.

2. Be realistic! This goes with the first tip. If a seller counters your initial offer, make sure you evaluate what is realistic. It's easy to say, let's increase the projected rent by $50 per month, or let's reduce the reserve for maintenance or vacancy to offset the higher sale price. Don't do it. Your numbers are conservative for a reason; to allow a little wiggle room for the unanticipated items that may come up.

3. Re-reflect on your short and long term goals. Make sure your offer and the opportunity are in alignment with what you are working to accomplish.

Finally, as you consider all of the factors I mentioned, be sure to check your gut feeling or intuition. If something doesn't "feel" right or if it seems as if you have to force something for the opportunity to make sense, take this as a huge red flag to evaluate if you really want to move forward with the opportunity. In our private group, we have developed a community where we share and help each other consider the opportunities at hand. If you want to participate, visit www.CourtneyMKing.com/join.

7

STEP THREE

PREPARING TO CLOSE ON THE OPPORTUNITY

Now that you and your agent have identified the right opportunity that will get you to freedom from your student loan debt or success with any other long and short term goals you've set, now it's time to negotiate and get your offer accepted. This is where your agent will get to work their "magic." Throughout this process, your agent will be your guide. Keep in mind, you may have to analyze quite a few opportunities until you find the one. This is normal. Stick to your guns and your goals and be patient.

Once the seller has accepted your offer, it's VERY important to get a home inspection. An inspector will thoroughly comb through the property, so you have a very clear picture of what you are buying. At the showing, you saw most things, but the inspector will dive deeper. Once you have the inspection report you will want to consult with both your agent and general contractor and/or property manager to get an idea of repairs (maybe ones that you didn't anticipate) and use the estimated costs of those repairs to negotiate a concession in lieu of repair or actually ask the seller to complete these. I'll leave that up to your agent or broker to advise you on the best course of action.

Once all of the terms have been negotiated with the seller, your mortgage lender will start to process your loan. Keep in mind that they will ask you for a TON of documents; it's par for the course! While they do their processes, it would be a good idea for you to shop around for those variables that you can control like insurance and property management (if you haven't selected a manager already), which may allow you to save money and increase your overall cash flow. At this moment, it would be wise to revisit your projections for the opportunity (i.e., the spreadsheets in the earlier chapter) to continue to verify that you are in alignment with your goals. Do you see the pattern? It's always good to continue to revisit your goals; after all, we're trying to get you free from your student loan debt!

Property management

I mentioned earlier in the book that property management can make or break your investment opportunity. This includes if you self-manage your property or you hire a company. Since I know the ins-and-outs of property management, my first and foremost recommendation is to hire a property manager. No, it's not because that's my business. I have literally talked to and done business with people that have tried to self-manage and drove themselves and their property into the ground. Property management is a relatively inexpensive price to pay for PEACE OF MIND! Do you want to wake up to 2AM calls for a plumbing backup? Do you want to be the person that has to file to evict someone that is not paying? Do you even know where to begin with your state and local landlord-tenant laws? While it is good to educate yourself, a property manager has both the experience and education to not only educate you on the lay of the land but also take it off your hands. For me, it frees up my time, which is a precious commodity that I can't get back, and it's PRICE-LESS. I know you're asking, "Courtney, do you have a property manager?" The answer is YES, King Realty & Management Inc. Be sure to re-read Chapter Five where I talked about how to select the right property manager for you.

If you have your mind already made up that you want to self-manage your property instead of hiring a professional, I commend you! It is possible, and it does, in fact, save you money and increase your cash flow. Soon, I will publish a book on how to self-manage. Be sure to visit www. CourtneyMKing.com for updates. In the meantime, be sure that you thoroughly research your local landlord-tenant laws. Many cities across the United States are implementing "rental registration programs" that require a city inspector to inspect the property before you rent it out. It's important to stay current on all these things to minimize your liability. Last but not least, keep in mind that this is a business! This is not your personal home. I say that because I have seen first-hand how tenants will take advantage of an owner that self-manages their property.

Make ready

The term make-ready describes the general contractor work that is needed to get the property in the "move-in ready" shape. Your property management team likely already has contacts and crews that perform this work. At King Realty & Management Inc., we have an in-house maintenance crew that does all our make-ready work. If you decide to self-manage, be sure to consult with your agent or broker as they too likely haver contractor referrals that will help you.

At a minimum, there are basic compliance rules set by your state and local laws. For example, in Texas, they require keyless locking devices on all doors that lead to outside and the garage. They also require a peephole on these same doors if there is not a window adjacent or if the door to the exterior is not glass. Additionally, in Texas, you must rekey (or change the locks/keys that open all doors) after each occupant. These are the necessary make-ready items that I had to do on Michael Drive and that I recommend to all of my clients.

The next thing I focus on in the make-ready process is how to "bulletproof" the property; how to make it virtually indestructible to a tenant. Again, this is part of the long-term items that I focus on so that I can reduce my expenses over time. With Michael Drive, the house had laminate flooring throughout (no carpet), which was heaven sent! By replacing carpet with some sort of hard-surface flooring, you don't have the issue of carpet getting stained or damaged by kids and pets, which reduces your expenses over time. If you want a basic make-ready checklist be sure to visit my website.

The two keys to renting the property quickly and for top dollar are PRICE and CONDITION! In my 9+ years of experience, it boils down to this. As you work with your property manager or agent/broker to lease the property make sure that you are in alignment with what the market is doing in that immediate area. You have all of this data already from when you analyzed the opportunity in Chapter Six. In terms of condition, making sure the property is landscaped, clean and ready for move-in shows prospective tenants that you care about the property and also how you expect them to maintain it. My dad always said, "Ugly houses bring ugly tenants!" By focusing on the condition and making it move-in ready, you increase the quality of the tenant you attract.

8

STEP FOUR

YOU'RE A LANDLORD, NOW WHAT?

Congrats! You are now a landlord, now what? By now, you should have already decided if you will hire a property manager or self-manage. In the last chapter, I talked about the HUGE benefits of a property manager, so we'll assume that you will go that route. The first step is to set the expectations for you and your manager. This comes as you discuss their procedures for communicating with you when there are issues at the home or with the tenant. Next, it's a good idea to make sure that you also have expectations for yourself in terms of response times to your manager and what kind of landlord you want to be. Here's a quick note, I've dealt with so many different "types" of landlords. I will say the "uptight" and/or emotionally driven ones are always stressed out, but the ones that look at this as a business and understand that there may be future, unanticipated expenses that come up and have budgeted adequately for those have a more positive experience as a landlord. I'll let you choose which one you want to be.

Since you're reading this book, it's safe to say that you plan on using the cash flow to pay down or pay off your student loan debt (or any other debt for that matter). Be sure to continue to look at your cash flow and goals on both a monthly and semi-annual and annual basis and make adjustments. While your mortgage is not likely to change (unless you are on an adjustable-rate), the other variables that may change are the cost of taxes and insurance and HOA dues (if you are in a homeowners association). Make sure you are proactive in monitoring those costs and shopping around as needed, particularly for insurance. When it comes to monitoring property taxes, your agent/broker can pull annual reports to ensure that the assessed property tax value is in alignment with the market value. In Texas, if your market value is less than what the taxing entity has, there is a window annually where you can protest the taxes in hopes that they reduce the value and thus your annual property tax expense. For all of my Texas landlords, visit www. CourtneyMKing.com/tax for tips on protesting.

Record keeping

If you are using a property manager, they must be keeping track of your income and expenses on a monthly and annual basis through regular reports. After all, this helps to ensure your property is performing as it should, and if not, you can use the data to adjust. These records are also vital so that you can take full advantage of the tax benefits associated with being a landlord. In addition to the day-to-day income and expense records, it's also vital to keep a record of the rental applications and lease agreements on file. Each state varies on how long you must keep those records.

For the folks self-managing, be sure to subscribe to some sort of service (web-based platform) that allows you to keep everything in an online portal. These services also allow you to receive online rent payments from your tenant. Be sure to visit my site www.CourtneyMKing.com/selfmanage for recommendations on the best platforms for self-managing.

Healthy landlord mindsets

Earlier I mentioned that you have the choice to be a different "type of landlord." This goes along with landlord mindsets. Here are a few that will help you have a positive experience as a landlord.

1. *New tenant "troubles."* Since you have never occupied the property you purchased, nine times out of ten, a new tenant will submit a maintenance request for issues that didn't come up in the inspection or the make-ready. This is VERY normal. When you understand this to start, you won't freak out when that request comes in. This usually happens when someone moves in, and if you tackle it early on it shouldn't be an issue after the first month. Tenants will frequently "test" the landlord. If their request is cosmetic in nature you may want to have your manager document the repair needed. If it's not cosmetic, bite the bullet and have them complete the repair. This will help you, and your tenant start off on the "right" foot. Remember, these types of expenses are usually tax-deductible.

2. *Importance of preventative maintenance.* Some investors have an "I'm going to ride it until the wheels fall off" mentality. This virtually means, if something is only slightly broken/damaged, they are going to let it be until it absolutely has to be repaired. Time and time again, I have seen this approach cost investors lots of money. By doing

preventative maintenance like servicing the HVAC semi-annually or having the property sprayed for pests annually are easy and relatively inexpensive things to do, which will save you money over time.

3. *Communication with your property manager.* They say "communication is key" in relationships. This is no different than with your property manager. At a minimum, your property manager should be communicating with you at least once a month (usually your monthly statement). If you have any questions, always communicate with your manager and document in writing (e-mail is fine). Since you already established expectations with your property manager this shouldn't be a big deal, but if in doubt just reach out to them.

9

STEP FIVE

PAYING OFF YOUR STUDENT LOAN DEBT

At this moment, I walked you through the steps from start to finish on how you purchase an investment property like the one I first bought on Michael Drive. By now, you have (or will have shortly) a tenant in place so that you can begin earning a monthly cash flow. I highly recommend that you establish a separate bank account specifically for this property. This will help you when it comes to tracking all income and expenses.

Each month that your tenant pays rent, they are paying your monthly mortgage (PITI – principal interest taxes and insurance), and all excess is your monthly cash flow. What do you do with it? By now, I've become a broken record, but I will say this one last time; you want to revisit your goals and make sure you are consulting with a tax professional throughout this process. In an ideal world that monthly cash flow will cover your student loan payment. However, if it doesn't, you may have to pair a piece of your income (salary) with the cash flow to make your full payment. This is still better than you coming out of your own pocket which would be the case if you didn't have the property. What I did was pay my usual monthly payment out of the income I received as a teacher and use the cash flow to make <u>additional</u> principal-only payments. While the regular payment going to principal and interest (and mostly interest at that), the extra payment was a way to aggressively pay down the loan and save quite a bit in interest over time. As you first get started it may be wise to set aside some of the cash flow in a separate saving account for this property to cover any future maintenance or vacancy expenses. This may cut into the amount of your extra principal payment, but you'll be glad you did this because you will be prepared if or when you have an unforeseen expense arise.

The long game

You will see the most gains in terms of paying off your student loan debt entirely over the long haul! Initially, you benefit through the monthly cash flow. Also, while your tenant is paying the monthly mortgage, you are building equity over time. This is something many investors don't always consider because you don't necessarily see that unless you go comparing what you owe to the value of the property. That is indeed important as the equity you continue to grow could also provide lots of benefits that we don't cover here.

You have the option to continue to pay down/off your student loan debt using the monthly cashflow OR depending on what the market does in your area, you may consider selling the property like I did, to pay your debt off in full. Since I bought the Michael Drive property in a down market, the amount of appreciation (increase in value) that I experienced over the year and half that I owned the property was INSANE! This just highlights the importance of having the right team to guide you in this process. Be sure you are staying in touch with your agent or broker or your property manager about the ongoing changes in the market. This may dictate the route that you take with your investment.

The payoff

In early 2013 one of our long-term clients (an out-of-state investor who had investment properties that we managed at the time) was looking for another rental property to add to his portfolio. In the process of sending various opportunities to him, I also presented Michael Drive as an opportunity. By this time, I was on my second tenant renting for $1295 per month with very minimal maintenance issues while I had owned it. Whereas I purchase the property in 2011 for $68,000, the house was worth over $90,000 (that is appreciation). The fact that I had a tenant in place also added to the appeal for this client. In full transparency, I told him that with the sale of the property, I would be able to pay off my remaining student loan debt and put money in my pocket. He agreed, and the rest is history.

After a little over five years and nine months since graduating from college, my student loan debt was completely paid off! I hope that you can do the same with this same strategy! While it's beyond this book and my expertise, please note that if you sell your property, you must also consider the tax implications (capital gains), so be sure to consult with a tax professional BEFORE you decide to sell. There are legal ways to minimize your tax liability in the process.

Since my immediate goal was to pay off my student loan debt in full using this asset, that was the right path for me. However, if I had kept this as an investment that house today as I write this book, would be closer to $150,000! Yes, I could kick myself for selling it, however, because it was in alignment with my goals, I won't do that. Since then, I've continued to invest in different cash-flowing opportunities that pay for other debt or liability, not to mention these opportunities have helped me to build 800+ credit scores, which makes pursuing other opportunities in life and business that much easier. As you complete one goal, be sure to continue to set other goals that will help you to continue to grow.

Adding to your portfolio

After you reach success with your first investment property, why not add to your portfolio? I continue to do this personally and I also help clients to do the same. You can use the same practical method outlined in this book to grow your portfolio and increase your overall passive income. As you do this, continue to evaluate not only your long and short-term goals but also the real estate market cycle. I'd love to hear about your success! Visit www.CourtneyMKing.com/testimonial to share your story!

CONCLUSION

(AND HOW YOU CAN APPLY THIS SAME PROCESS WITH OTHER DEBT YOU MAY HAVE)

In his "Rich Dad" series, Robert Kiyosaki talks about the importance of financial intelligence and the fundamentals of "good debt" and "Other People's Money" (OPM). He explains that good debt is any debt that puts money back in your pocket. Good debt is also a type of OPM. OPM is another strategy where you put other people's money to work to increase your overall return on investment.

The concept of OPM was first introduced in the 1700s by Adam Smith's book The Wealth of Nations. It is essentially what banks do every day with the money that you have sitting there. They use your (and others') money to lend out at a higher interest rate to earn more. At the end of the day, that's what these student loan lenders are doing as well!

In this book, I highlighted how I used OPM to purchase the investment property on Michael Drive. I also used OPM (the tenant's rent payment) to pay down/off the loan, build equity, and pay off all of my student loan debt at the same time!

Here's a summary of the step-by-step process outlined.

1. Examine your present financial situation (credit, income, student loan debt balance, etc.) and start setting goals
2. Find your team (Agent/Broker, Lender, Property Manager)
3. Locate the right opportunity to get you to your goals
4. Closing on the opportunity
5. Being a landlord and the proper landlord mindset
6. Paying down and paying off your student loan debt

Now that you have completed this once time, you can also use this to tackle any other liability that you have and continue to pursue financial freedom. Most of all, you're not limited to just one opportunity at a time! Let me pause by interjecting a quick note on the pitfalls of overleveraging. If you decide to purchase multiple properties using some sort of financing, you will want to consult with a lender and financial advisor to ensure that you're not overleveraged. In the most simplified terms, being overleveraged means that you carry so much debt that you are not able to make the payments-especially if something drastic happens to the housing market or the economy. After all, that is one of the risks in investing in real estate.

One thing that I continue to do is buy multiple properties to increase my overall monthly cash-flow. While this may not be for everyone, one of my goals is to continue to use this strategy to continue to build more passive income, which will free me up to continue to live out the purpose for which God sent me here to this earth. If you also decide to add additional properties to your portfolio, you have the opportunity to double, triple, or even quadruple your monthly cash flow, which can cover any other liabilities (bills, car notes, etc.) or add to your savings or retirement accounts. Despite the regulations on how many "traditional" mortgages you can have in your name, there are also other creative financing strategies that will allow you to add to your portfolio and continue to build your cash flow. Feel free to visit www.CourtneyMKing.com/join to join our community and learn about more strategies that will help you.

The objection

Now that you're on the last chapter there may be a few objections ringing in your head. "...but I currently rent an apartment...but I'm not a homeowner....but...." The list can go on and on. The fact is I was not a homeowner when I purchased my first investment. Who says you must be a homeowner anyway? What if the investment can offset what you pay for an apartment or any of your other regular living expenses? I encourage you to pause these thoughts, re-examine your goals and look at the bigger picture.

Re-evaluating your team

Finally, as you continue in this journey of freedom from student loans, you may need to regularly re-evaluate your team. With the evolution of business, sometimes service providers change, and such changes may not be conducive to how you do business or in alignment with your goals. It happens! Be sure to monitor this as closely as you monitor your investments to make sure that you are getting what you need in terms of service, information, and communication.

Learn, leverage, legacy

Thank you for picking up this book and joining me on my journey of paying off my student loan debt. If you are not in the position of doing what I did, don't be discouraged! There's no judgment! I encourage you to start educating yourself and preparing your finances and your credit to be able to make these types of investments in the future. While I know it can be scary, taking the first step can have HUGE positive implications for your family, kids (or future kids if you don't presently have any), and generations to come. I know firsthand how the bondage of student loan debt can be downright paralyzing, but it doesn't have to be.

Hosea 4:6 (KJV) says, "My people are destroyed for lack of knowledge..." I encourage you to keep seeking knowledge, keep seeking an understanding of how you can break free of this machine that is called student loan debt. We'd love for you to join our community of others that are actively working on doing the same. Please visit www. CourtneyMKing.com/start to begin taking the first step toward FREEDOM from student loan debt and change the course of history for you, your family and future generations!

End

NOTES

2. Student Loan Debt in the United States

1. https://www.nbcnews.com/news/us-news/student-loan-statistics-2019-n997836
2. https://www.federalreserve.gov/publications/2018-economic-well-being-of-us-households-in-2017-student-loans.htm
3. https://www.nbcnews.com/news/us-news/student-loan-statistics-2019-n997836
4. https://www.cbo.gov/publication/45383

ABOUT THE AUTHOR

Courtney King is a graduate from Pepperdine University and a Texas real estate broker and investor. She is a serial entrepreneur and owner of King Realty & Management Inc., a residential real estate brokerage services the Dallas-Fort Worth and Houston metropolitan areas. Her passion is to pursue God's purpose for her life and share her experiences, and the wisdom passed down from her parents to motivate and help people fulfill their calling and purpose. Courtney currently resides in Houston, Texas, and is actively growing her businesses while giving back to the community through her family's non-profit, King Sovereign Farms. You can learn more about Courtney by visiting her website at www.CourtneyMKing.com and following her on social media @KingRealtyTexas on Facebook and Instagram, @MillennialVsMachine on Instagram, and @KingRealtyTX on YouTube.

www.ingramcontent.com/pod-product-compliance
Lightning Source LLC
Chambersburg PA
CBHW071644040426

42452CB00009B/1759